HeroRATs

Written by Jenny Feely

Flying Start
to Literacy®

T0342926

Contents

Introduction

In the cool of the morning, a giant rat is at work in the grounds of an abandoned hospital. He is with his trainer. The rat energetically sniffs his way through the grass. Suddenly he stops, puts his nose to the ground and scratches at the dirt.

This rat has found one of the dangerous landmines buried under the ground during a recent war. These landmines have prevented the local people from using the hospital. The trainer uses a clicker to make a click sound. When the rat hears this sound, he runs to the trainer and receives his reward for finding the landmine – a piece of banana.

HeroRATs are light in weight. They are too light to set off a landmine.

Mac the HeroRAT receives a banana reward after finding a landmine.

Mac is known as a HeroRAT, because he works hard to help people be safe and to have better lives.

The landmines that Mac finds are carefully excavated and safely destroyed. Soon the hospital building will be safe for people again.

How did rats like Mac come to be heroes? Who saw the potential in rats and took the time and effort needed to train them? The answer is Bart Weetjens. As a child, Bart loved animals and as an adult, he saw a way to work with rats to make the world a better place.

CHAPTER 1

Meet Bart Weetjens

Bart Weetjens is a Dutch man with a passion for helping others and a great love for animals. When these two things came together, a wonderful plan was born. Weetjens said:

As a child, I had two passions. One was a passion for rodents. I had all kinds of rats, mice, hamsters, gerbils, squirrels. You name it, I bred it. I also had a passion for Africa. I learnt a lc about African cultures and soon started travelling there.

But when Bart travelled through Africa, he discovered the problem of landmines. Bart wanted to help people in war-torn countries. He was interested in making the world a better place and in everyone having equal chances.

In my opinion, this problem of landmines needed to be dealt with first.

Landmines
In the past 20 years, 65 million landmines have been buried in fields in countries where there are wars.

Bart Weetjens and Chavez, an African giant-pouched HeroRAT

The problem of landmines

Landmines are small bombs that are buried under the ground. These small bombs are planted during wars to stop people from crossing a part of the country or to protect places from being attacked. Stepping on a landmine or driving a vehicle over a landmine can trigger a deadly explosion.

After a war has ended, landmines are often left buried under the ground. The yellow markers in this photograph show where landmines have been found and destroyed.

When wars are over, the landmines are not removed. They remain buried under the ground. No one knows exactly where landmines are buried so finding them is difficult and dangerous. It takes a long time to find the landmines and remove them.

Areas where people think landmines might be buried cannot be used for farming, housing or any other purpose. Important resources such as electricity and water supplies cannot be repaired if there are landmines buried near them. Even buildings such as schools and hospitals cannot be used because landmines may be buried nearby.

Thinking about the problem

When Bart Weetjens thought about how to solve the
problem of landmines, he didn't immediately think
of training rats. One day, he read that rodents were
being trained to smell particular scents. This made him
wonder: could rats be trained to detect the scent of the
explosives in landmines?

From his years of raising pet rats, Weetjens knew that rats were intelligent and had a keen sense of smell. They were easily trained and would do the same task over and over. But what kind of rats would be best to use and how would they need to be trained?

Weetjens began a research project to find out. He tested a range of rats and developed a training program. He wanted his project to be run by people who lived in places affected by landmines. And he wanted it to be inexpensive.

He began the HeroRATs project and established an organisation that employs people from countries where the rats are needed. They train the rats and use them to find mines.

The organisation that Weetjens set up to train HeroRATs is called APOPO, which is an acronym of a Dutch name meaning Anti-Personnel Landmines Detection Product Development.
Mac is one of the many HeroRATs that APOPO has successfully trained to sniff out landmines.

Mac the rat

CHAPTER 2

The right rat for the job

Weetjens decided that African giant-pouched rats were best suited for the job. These rats are bigger than other rats. This makes them easier to work with and easier to see when they are moving in long grass sniffing for landmines.

Most importantly, these rats are not heavy enough to set off the landmines.

Weetjens chose the African giant-pouched rat to train as sniffer rats.

HeroRATs are trained to find landmines like this one.

Weetjens discovered that trained African giant-pouched rats were much faster than people at finding landmines. A HeroRAT can check an area the size of a tennis court in just 20 minutes. This task could take a deminer (a person with a metal detector) up to four days.

The rats found 100 per cent of the landmines in an area and they seemed happy to do the work. They would eagerly sniff out deadly bombs, if rewarded with food.

Training HeroRATs

It takes nine months to train a HeroRAT. During the training, the rats are very well treated. They have safe, comfortable nests to sleep in. They are well fed and they have regular vet checks. There are six steps to train a HeroRAT.

Step 1

A rat begins training when it is four weeks old. The first thing the rat needs to learn is that its trainer is friendly and safe. The trainer picks up the rat, plays with it and introduces it to many different smells.

Mac as a young rat with his trainer

This young rat is learning that when it hears the clicker, it will receive food.

Step 2

When the rat is six weeks old, it learns to associate getting a food reward with a click sound. The trainer uses a clicker to make a click sound at the same time as the rat is given a food reward. Weetjens said:

> The rats are very greedy and like to get treats. They will do anything for their treats.

Step 3

Once the rat knows that a click means food, it is ready to be trained to find a particular smell. The trainer exposes it to the target scent of the explosive TNT, hidden inside a tea ball placed on top of a table covered in dirt. When the rat goes to the target scent and sniffs at it for a few seconds, the trainer clicks and the rat gets a treat.

15

Step 4

After the rat has mastered finding the target scent, more tea balls are placed on an area of floor covered in dirt that the rat has to search systematically. Only some of the tea balls have the target scent. When the rat sniffs the target scent, the trainer clicks and gives the rat a food treat.

Step 5

The next step is finding buried tea balls. Instead of finding tea balls containing TNT that are on top of the dirt, they are now all buried underground. When the rat digs where the tea balls containing TNT are buried, it is rewarded with food.

This young rat has found the tea ball with the target smell.

This rat is learning to walk in a harness out in the open. This helps the rat to overcome its natural fear of being attacked.

Step 6

The rat is now ready for the test field where both fake and real landmines have been buried. The real landmines do not have triggers so they cannot explode. When the rat can successfully find all of the real landmines in a given area, it is ready for work.

CHAPTER 3

Off to work

Today, HeroRATs are working in countries in Africa and Asia.

Each morning, before it is too hot, the handler takes the HeroRAT to the area that needs to be cleared of landmines. The rat works for 20 minutes, sniffing all over the area. When the rat finds a mine, it digs into the dirt and the handler places a flag to mark the spot.

Clearing landmines

Since APOPO was founded in 1997, HeroRATs have helped clear more than 18,800 landmines in minefields in Africa and Asia. During this time, not one rat has been injured or died from landmines.

A deminer, someone who destroys landmines, identifies the exact position of a landmine, and then blows it up.

Then it is the turn of humans to finish off the job, while the rat rests. Deminers, people who destroy mines, use metal detectors to pinpoint exactly where the landmine is. The dirt around the landmine is carefully removed so the landmine is visible. Markers are placed around the landmine, clearly showing its location. At the end of the day, all the landmines in the field are safely destroyed.

19

Sam's community has been terrorised by hidden landmines left over from the war 30 years ago.

Sam's story

Sam is a cattle farmer in Mozambique.

My family lives near electricity pylons that were protected by landmines during the civil war. My friend was killed trying to retrieve his cow from this land. Sometimes we had to take risks and farm the land or cross it for a shortcut. Sometimes I found my children playing there.

Then APOPO arrived to clear the landmines. They used machines and landmine detection rats. At some pylons they found no landmines; at others there were many. We have lived in fear because we did not know where the landmines were buried. My children have lived with this fear all their lives.

APOPO is reducing this fear every day. Less than one year after arriving in the area, APOPO announced the all-clear. Our land is once again ours to farm and our children are safe.

A deminer shows some of the many weapons and landmines that have been found and removed from farming land.

CHAPTER 4

Weetjens has another idea

The success of the HeroRATs in detecting landmines made Weetjens wonder what else the rats could be trained to do. He turned his mind to the fight against a terrible disease called tuberculosis (TB).

Tuberculosis is a lung disease that kills more than one million people every year. There is a treatment available for people who become infected with TB, but it is important that they start treatment as soon as possible to increase their chances of being cured and to stop the spread of the disease.

A deadly disease

Tuberculosis is an infectious disease. Each year, it kills more people than any other infectious disease.

One third of the world's population is infected with TB. In 2014, 9.6 million people around the world became sick with TB and there were 1.5 million TB-related deaths worldwide.

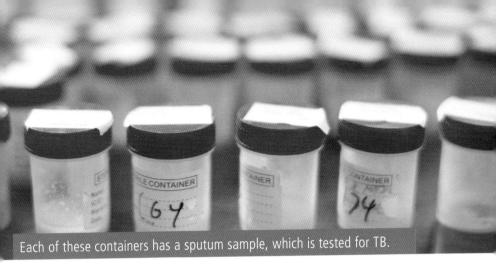

Each of these containers has a sputum sample, which is tested for TB.

Doctors diagnose whether a person has TB or not by collecting a sample of lung fluid called sputum. These samples are tested. If the sample is positive, this means that the person has TB and treatment can begin. If the sample is negative, then the person does not have TB.

But the sputum test is not always accurate. Only about half of patients with TB are successfully diagnosed using the sputum test.

Bart Weetjens wondered if rats could be trained to detect the smell of TB in the sputum samples.

HeroRATs can detect TB

Weetjens was right! APOPO has now successfully trained rats to detect the scent of TB in sputum samples.

The rats can screen more than 100 sputum samples in 20 minutes, a job that a person working in a lab would take up to four days to complete.

HeroRATs have identified more than 10,000 people who had TB but whose sputum test didn't pick it up. This has saved the life of each patient and those people that may have been infected if the patient had remained untreated.

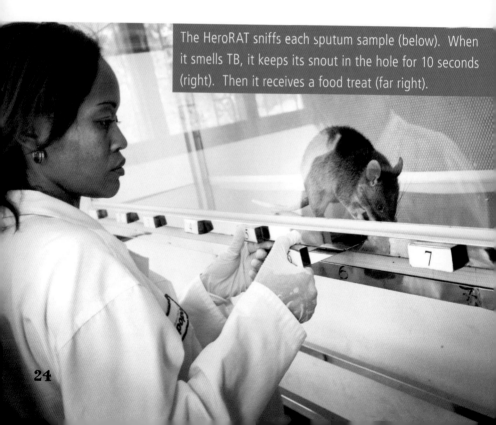

The HeroRAT sniffs each sputum sample (below). When it smells TB, it keeps its snout in the hole for 10 seconds (right). Then it receives a food treat (far right).

24

Claudi and his grandmother

Claudi's story

Claudi is six years old and lives in Tanzania.

*In 2014, I became very sick so my grandmother took me
to the doctor who examined me and suspected that I
had TB. At the clinic we also met Lulu, a volunteer from
APOPO. She has had TB and gives people advice about
it. She helped me to give my sputum sample. The clinic
tried to detect what was wrong with me, but they couldn't
find anything.*

After a while I felt worse. My little sister got sick, too. I was coughing a lot and feeling so sick that I couldn't go to school. Then one day the clinic found out that I did have TB because my sputum sample had been sent to APOPO. My TB was identified by a HeroRAT. Lulu came to my house to tell me I had TB and brought medicine to treat my little sister and me.

Thanks to the rats and the people at APOPO, we are both well again and I can go back to school.

Now that Claudi no longer has TB, he can return to school.

CHAPTER 5

Rats in retirement

Bart Weetjens and APOPO have a strong belief that all living things need to be treated with dignity and care. So they look after the HeroRATs very well for their whole lives. This is something that APOPO takes very seriously.

In the wild, African giant-pouched rats live for up to three years. The HeroRATs live for six to eight years.

Sunscreen is put on the rat's tail and ears to stop sunburn.

When a HeroRAT gets older, it becomes more easily tired and less interested in working. When this happens, the rat is retired from work. It will have a cozy nest to live in for the rest of its life, and receive a carefully balanced diet, regular exercise and routine visits by vets. It will be left in peace, surrounded by its friends, until it dies.

Conclusion

Making a difference in a world filled with difficult problems can seem overwhelming. But when people like Bart Weetjens put their minds and their hearts to work, amazing things can be achieved.

Bart Weetjens and his HeroRATs are changing the world one sniff at a time, making it a safer, healthier and happier place.

And all thanks to a young boy who loved rats!

APOPO operates in several countries in Africa and Southeast Asia.

What can you do?

As people all around the world have learnt about the important and amazing work done by Bart Weetjens and his team at APOPO, there have been many offers of support. Some people volunteer their time. Others raise money for APOPO. And some join the Adopt a HeroRAT program. Information about how you can help can be found at: www.apopo.org